Vagabond Verses

A collection of poems that wander through
diverse themes

SHASHI BISHT

BookLeaf
Publishing

India | USA | UK

Made with ❤ on the BookLeaf Publishing Platform
www.bookleafpub.in
www.bookleafpub.com

Dedication

To my parents for their selfless devotion, guidance, support and shaping me into a confident, capable and compassionate individual. They celebrated my triumphs, comforted me in times of need and encouraged me to chase my dreams..

To my dearest son, Atharva...
Who's the sole reason of me becoming a poetess.. . Your constant encouragement made me realise the part of me I was leaving to wither away.

To my beloved husband, Deepak
Thank you for coming into my life and filling it with rainbow colours. As an Army wife, now I see this world through a totally different lens.Your unconditional love has inspired me to push beyond my limits and to never give up on my goals.

With all my heart, now and forever.......

Preface

The poetess in me was born in a remote area in Arunachal Pradesh where my husband was commanding one of the elite battalion of the Indian Army. I along with my son was staying with him as the school was running online due to the pandemic.

Once a poem recitation competition at my son's school motivated me to write my first poem as I don't wanted him to recite an age old easily available poem over Internet. And as the saying goes "Necessity is the Mother of Invention" I put my thoughts into words and finally they became poems.

My collection of poems in "Vagabond Verses" are the various emotions felt since then based on various experiences .

May the reader find solace, connect, comfort and inspiration within these pages.

-Shashi Bisht

Acknowledgements

I am deeply grateful to the many individuals who have supported me throughout the writing of this book.

First and foremost ,My Son Atharva, who first recognised the poetess in me and encouraged me to take this seriously. My husband Deepak, for being my in-house critic and admirer.

I would also like to express my heartfelt thanks to my senior ladies and gal pals from Army fraternity for always encouraging me to write more. Their constant appreciation truly motivated me to embark my journey into the literary world.

I am also grateful to the team at Book Leaf publishing for their support and expertise in bringing this book to publication.Truly appreciate them for fulfilling dreams of many budding authors like me.

Sincerely,
Shashi Bisht

1. अस्तित्व से भेंट

न जाने ज़िंदगी की कशमकश में,
कहाँ उलझे रह गए ।
बुने थे ख़्वाब ढेर सारे,
जाने क्यों अधूरे रह गए?

देख दूसरे का स्वप्न साकार ,
मन पुलकित हो जाता है।
पर ,अपूर्ण अपने स्वप्नों को याद कर ,
इक कोलाहल सा मच जाता है।।

क्या केवल गुणी होना ही है काफ़ी?
या क़िस्मत भी खेल दिखाती है ।
देख, विजेता को सिंहासन पर बैठे,
हर शंका ओझल हो जाती है।।

कैसा होगा वह क्षण ?
जब स्वप्न मेरा साकार होगा।।
इक इच्छा पूर्ति संग,
क्या नवीन स्वप्न का निर्माण होगा?

सुलझाऊँगी अब उलझे धागे,
महत्व स्वयं का जान गई हूँ ।
पूर्ण होंगे अब स्वप्न अनगिनत,
अस्तित्व "मैं "अपना पहचान गई हूँ ।।

2. Threads Of Unity

I love my country for its diversity,
As its beauty lies in its variety.

We are the pioneers of Buddhism and Yoga,
We are the one that taught the world Ayurveda.

Different seasons come and go,
Many festivals to celebrate in a row.

The nature boasts diverse flora and fauna,
Makes our country a colourful arena.

Citizen proudly don their native attire,
A quality of our culture that I truly admire.

People speak multiple languages and tones,
The visitors find it unique and are mind blown.

To face new challenges is in our nature,
Together we always ready for any such adventure.

Blessed are we to live in harmony and peace,
To remain united in diversity with such ease.

It's the diversity that makes us great and strong,
Weakens our foes and prove them wrong.

3. माँ

एक शब्द ,में निहित,
मेरा अखिल संसार है ।।
हूँ ,तुम्हारी भाग "मैं",
इसका मुझे अभिमान है ।।

चलना, बोलना और पढ़ना ,
तुमने ही तो ,है सिखाया ।।
कुंठा हाथ लगने पर,
मनोबल ,तुमने ही बढ़ाया ।।

मेरी प्रत्येक,उपलब्धि पर,
सहसा पुलकित ,तुम हों उठती ।।
और मेरे, साकार स्वप्नों में,
तुम स्वयं को, ही देखती।।

तुम्हें गौरवान्वित करना,
रहा सदा ही, ध्येय मेरा ।।
मेरा सहज व्यक्तित्व है,
फल, तुम्हारे परिश्रम का ।।

छोड़ तुम्हें, ससुराल जाना,
था विषम , मेरे लिये ।।
पर नवीन संसार रचना,
भी सिखाया, तुम्हीं ने ।।

जब स्वयं मैं "मॉं"बनी,
सन्निकट तुमसे हो गई ।।
तुम्हारे अनुभवों कि छाँव में,
वात्सल्य पथ पर,अग्रसर हो गई ।।

तुम्हें प्यार से "नंदु" पुकारना,
फिर तुम्हारा खिल-खिलाना ।।
नित्य तुमसे बात करना,
किसी सुखद-अनुभूति से,कम नहीं ।।

जानती हो मॉं, कब,
हिय हर्षित हो उठता है ।।
जब लोग मुझसे यह कहें,
मुझमें तुम्हारा "प्रतिबिंब "दिखता है ।।

4. Nurturing Souls

To become a parent is equally gratifying and
challenging,
But to raise them takes insurmountable patience and
caring.

Accept your child with all their flaws and strengths,
And witness their immense potential reaching infinite
lengths.

Believe your child as many of their feelings remain
unspoken,
This will help them in overcoming the feelings of
forsaken.

Spend quality time in a gadget free space,
As this will create memories that they will forever
embrace.

Communicate with your child even if their queries seem
far from reality,

As it will build self esteem and help them discover their
identity.

Learning is more experiential and not just always
theoretical,
Just facilitate that process as the knowledge gained will
be elemental.

Honour your child with respect as they are the future of
mankind,
This will assist in building a better world that will be
mindful and kind.

We all have our individual journeys and have to tread
path's of our own,
Join your child on their journey while you being present
at your parent zone.

Dear parents they are the fruits of your love and
emotions,
And not tools to achieve your unconsummated dreams
and ambitions.

Tend your garden with love and care and see your
flowers bloom,
Nurture their real needs and watch them spread their
perfume.

5. बीस सालों का यह सफ़र

बीस सालों का यह सफ़र ।
सिर्फ़ तुमने ही तय ,नहीं किया है प्रिये।।

तुम्हारे सपनों की उड़ान में।
मैं भी ,बराबर की भागीदार रही हूँ प्रिये।।

तुमसे परिणय सूत्र में बंधकर।
मैं भी ,देश को समर्पित हो गयी प्रिये।।

तुम संग एक नवीन संसार रचते हुए।
"यूनिट" सा एक प्यारा परिवार ,मैंने और पाया प्रिये।।

पीस/ फील्ड की सिलसिलेवार पोस्टिंग में।
ख़ुशी ख़ुशी मैंने कई "आशियाने "सजायें प्रिये।।

अपने पहले नाम को भी त्याग कर।
तुम्हारे उपनाम को सहर्ष स्वीकारा मैंने प्रिये।।

तुम देश के प्रति अपनी जिम्मेदारी निभा सको।
इसलिये घर की सारी जिम्मेदारी ,मैंने उठाई प्रिये।।

घर के बच्चे और बड़ों का ध्यान रखते।
कई बार ,अपना ख्याल रखना भी ,मैं भूली प्रिये।।

तुम्हारी छुट्टी होती त्योहार से कम नहीं ,हमारे लिये।
और प्रत्येक उत्सव रहता नीरस ,तुम बिन ,प्राण -प्रिये।।

जीवन यात्रा होती कुछ अलग ही ।
अगर ना रास्ते ,हमारे मिलते प्रिये।।

पर गर्व है मुझे ,बनी तुम्हारी जीवन संगिनी मैं।
अन्यथा एक "फ़ौजी की बीवी "कहलाने का गर्व कैसे पाती प्रिये।।

6. The Song Of Soul

God is not an abstract, intangible entity,
He is the one that possesses all opulence unlimitedly.

He descend to annihilate the miscreants and reestablish
the religion,
One can only realise him through undivided devotion.

As law books govern our life as citizens of the country,
So does the Vedic scriptures do,to uplift the human
society.

Bhagwad-Gita is a timeless classic of wisdom and not
just a primeval story,
It's a summum bonum of spiritual truth with an
enthralling history.

The body lives a degraded life dedicated to animalistic
desires and goal,
Awaken your self consciousness and become ONE with
the whole.

The soul simply follows the Law of Transmigration,
It doesn't discriminate on the basis of caste, creed and
religion.

So unleash yourself from the miserable bondage of the
Law of Karma,
Surrender and engage yourself to the devotional service
of Lord Krishna..

7. रेशम की डोर

आज फिर, वह उत्सव है आया ,
नम ये चक्षु हो गए ।
स्मरण कर बचपन कि स्मृतियाँ,
हिय भावुक कर गए ।।

क्या कहूँ बचपन था कैसा,
तीन कि ,लाड़ली 'मैं ' एक।
पलकों में ,सबके पली 'मैं',
पाईं ख़ुशियाँ, जग की अनेक।।

ज्येष्ठ भ्राता के लिए,
सदा रही पुत्री समान।
हो समस्त इच्छाएँ पूरी,
सदैव रखा ,उन्होंने ध्यान ।।

मंझले भ्राता ,कि क्या कहूँ,
रहे सदा वो प्रेरणा स्रोत ।
आज मेरे व्यक्तित्व में,
है उनका ,वृहत सहयोग ।।

कनिष्ठ भ्राता हैं 'मस्त मौला '
समग्र बचपन बीता उनके संग।
झगड़ते रहते थे कभी हम,
आज हैं ,घनिष्ठ भीत हम।।

आज कोसों दूर हैं पर,
दिल अभी भी पास हैं ।
रेशम कि डोर से बंधा ,
ये भाई बहन का प्यार है ।।

युगों युगों से चली आ रही,
परम्परा ये महान है।
जहां इक डोरी से जुड़ा,
असीम बंधन प्रगाढ़ है ।।

8. Slumber's Solace

SLEEP is not just a state of slumber,
It's your portal to infinite wonders.

Howsoever challenging your day had gone,
It always gives a promise, for an encouraging dawn.

You may be stuck with some illness today,
But a profound sleep,could mystically take it away.

When you get excited for those novel beginnings,
It charges you to kickstart the nearing innings.

Whenever traveling to far off distance,
Dose off to abbreviate the span,in an instance.

Don't delay your humble sleep,
As it's a gateway to feelings,embedded too deep.

So snuggle into your comfy-cozy bed,
Let the night take away, all your stress.

९. गणपति बप्पा मोरया

भाद्रपद की चतुर्थी को,
हुआ जिनका अवतरण ।
गौरी-सुत गणेश को,
मेरा हर्षातिरेक अभिनंदन।।

निराकार,प्रतीकात्मक छवि जिनकी,
रुद्र प्रिय ,भालचंद्र , लंबोदर ।
वक्रतुण्ड ,एकाक्षर ,चतुर्भुज,
आखुरत,सुमुखा, दामोदर।।

उत्पन्न हुए संरचना से जो,
मृत्युंजय क्रोध से हुए निर्जीव ।
पुनर्जीवित हुए गजमुख लगाकर ,
गिरिजा नंदन ,मोदक प्रिय ।।

रिद्धि-सिद्धि के हैं यह स्वामी,
शुभ-लाभ के पिता महान ।
धैर्य,विवेक,लेखन के स्वामी ,
महाकाव्य के रचनाकार।।

शिव दर्शन अभिलाषी परशुराम ने ,
जब किया दिव्य परशु से वार
रखा मान उस अस्त्र प्रहार का,
ऐसे एकदंत,अलौकिक आकार ।।

मात-पिता की परिक्रमा कर,
दिया विश्व को परम ज्ञान।
ऐसे अग्रपूज्य ,गणाधिपति को,
मेरा कोटि-कोटि प्रणाम।।

10. Ephemeral Skies

Sometimes grey with murky thoughts.
Sometimes powdery with vacuous thoughts.

Sometimes airier like a cotton ball,
Wandering to remoteness without a fall.

Sometimes dense like a stone,
Coz of pondering of varied tones.

Sometimes a thought tiny as grain,
But often leading to unfading pain.

Sometimes fogged with protracted thoughts,
Often I wonder the nostalgia they brought.

O dear mind!!!!!what ever the cause,
Occasionally lemme enjoy the calm and pause.

11. जय कन्हैया लाल की

झूमो,नाचो ,गाओ मिलके,
हर्ष उत्सव है आया।
अराजकता को दूर भगाने,
अवतरित हुए नंदलाला।।

जन्म दिया देवकी ने पर,
कहलाए यशोदानंदन।
बंसी धुन से हर ले सबको,
नटखट गोकुल नंदन।।

रास रचनाएँ राधा संग,
वृन्दावन में कान्हा ।
"त्याग" प्रेम की है परिभाषा,
कह गए बृज गोपाला।।

भरी सभा जब विपदा आई,
पुकारे सखा को पाँचाली ।
प्रकट हुए उद्धारक बनकर ,
लीलाधर सुदर्शन धारी।।

बन ,सारथी धनंजय के,
दिया भगवद् गीता सार।
"कर्म "सबसे बड़ा धर्म है,
है, मोक्ष प्राप्ति का द्वार।।

आओ,इस मंगल बेला पर,
कृष्ण भक्ति में रम जाए।
तेरा मेरा सब त्यागकर,
भवसागर तर जाए ।।

12. Mhow Musings

As our spouses are away,
Let's not waste this time in pondering and dismay.

As I know you & thou know me,
Let's spread together the bonhomie.

Let your heart win over your brain,
Shed the inhibition and drench in rain.

Sip the coffee and read more often,
As the Combat Library has plethora of option.

Join the hobby classes in Sugrahini ,
As learning expels away every monotony.

The Hub is a spot for fun and amusement ,
Ditch the mundane by watching a flick for
entertainment.

Stroll the pristine Avenues short or long,

Saunter alone or take your bestie along.

Cooking meals make you cry,
Give sabudana khichadi and vada pav a try.

Dress up in thy favourite hue,
As cavorting in DSOMI was prolonged due.

Zumba or Holistic yoga,whatever you do,
Get chiseled before the much awaited "FOREIGN TOUR"

Belle's femme's !!
Party together as much as you can,
As when husbands will arrive home,
The humdrum too shall come again.

13. बापू

सत्य अहिंसा सद्भावना,
जिनके मूल जीवन आधार।
साबरमती के संत को ,
प्रथानुकूल श्रद्धा सुमन आभार।।

युवावस्था की इक घटना से,
हुआ जन संघर्ष का उद्धार ।
नस्लीय भेदभाव को मिटाने,
बने अत्याचार के प्रतिकार।।

चम्पारण हो या दांडी यात्रा ,
सदैव अहिंसा नीति अपनाई ।
जगा जन-जन स्वराज की भावना,
"राष्ट्रपिता"की उपलब्धि पाई।।

सत्याग्रह को अस्त्र बनाकर,
किया हरिजन अस्पृश्य उत्थान ।
सर्वोदयी समाज की रचना कर ,
संरक्षकता मंत्र किया प्रदान।।

कर प्रचार प्रसार "खादी"का,
उपनिवेशवाद का किया बहिष्कार।
स्वयं चरखे पर सूत बुनकर ,
दिया "स्वदेशी स्वावलंबन"विचार।।

सादा-जीवन पद्धति जिनकी ,
सत्य-अहिंसा रही विचारधारा।
आध्यात्मिकता को अपनाकर,
विश्व राजनैतिक परिदृश्य बदल डाला।।

आओ बापू के सिद्धांतों को,
नित्य जीवन में अपनायें ।
सर्वोपरि देशहित भावना से,
स्वच्छ-स्वस्थ,उन्नत "राष्ट्र"बनाएँ ।।

14. Winter Repose

Winter is a season for retreat & contemplation,
Wintering prepares you for renewal and transformation.

Plants and animals don't fight the winter,
They adapt and endure as they lived the summer.

Winter is filled with quiet pleasures,
To dive into the world of literary chronicles.

It's the season of those candle-lit dinners,
To revitalise the passion and intimacy between the
lovers.

It's the season of feasting and merriment,
To enjoy the festivals of revelry and amusement.

It's the season for nostalgia and wistfulness,
To reflect and regain insight from the past experiences.

We all go through our personal winters,

In the form of grief, rejection, illness and failures.

Wintering sometimes do good to us,
As they are real, asking something from us.

So learn to invite the winter in,
As wintering prepares you to emerge again into the
spring.

15. मातृभूमि की पुकार

है, संघर्ष से भरी ,
ज़िंदगी तो क्या हुआ ।
कश्ती उसी कि पार लगी,
जो तूफ़ानों से लड़ गया ।।

आज टूटें और बिखरे ,
है, तो फिर क्या हुआ ।
बिन चट्टानों से भिड़े,
कब, शैलजा को अपना मार्ग मिला ।।

दौर ऐसा आएगा इक,
लक्ष्य धूमिल होने लगेगा ।
याद करना आप निंदा,
फिर उत्साह उमड़ने लगेगा ।।

चंद मुश्किलों के उद्देश्यतः,
निरुत्साहित मन न कर।
याद कर बलिदान वीरों का,
व्यर्थ अमूल्य जीवन न कर।।

दे गए तुझको धरोहर,
करके अपना सर्वस्व न्योछावर ।
मथ तू अपने अहंकारों को,
तब तो अमृत सोपान होगा ।।

आओ मिलकर ले ये प्रण,
शौर्य गाथा नई लिखेंगे ।
देश भक्ति कि लौ जलाकर,
प्रगति मार्ग प्रशस्त करेंगे ।।

16. Happy New Year

With great splendour and cheer,
Here comes the Nuevo year.
With zillion desires and none fear,
Let's embrace the novel year.

What started with radiant hunger,
Ebbed quickly in the bygone year.
Time to actualise those pending resolutions,
Achieve them all with utter dedication.

Loss bring grief ,anger and confusion
Accept ,heal and overcome frustration.
It's natural to feel all of these emotions,
Navigate this terrain and practice self compassion.

You might have missed varied prospects,
That lead to self doubt and introspects.
Its time to rebound with new magnitude,
Accrue resilience with sheer attitude .

You might had begun something new,
To reach somewhere YOU only knew.
It's time for you to hold on tight,
arrive your destination with unabridged might.

You might be feeling dejected and played,
From the closest,you got betrayed .
It's time to absolve and reconcile
Enlighten the soul to detach and unprejudice.

Don't be harsh and unkind to self,
Cease to embarrass and pity yourself.
Time for you to care and recover,
Mend the wrecked self-bond for ever.

New year is like a placid opportunity,
Grab it mindfully with grit and tenacity.
Fresh and scar-free as it may appear,
Make it memorable before it disappear.

Wishing everyone a wonderful year,
Joyful, blessed,thoughtful and clear.
May you be rapturous and whimsical,
May your life be refulgent and jovial.

17. वृहद महाकुंभ

आस्था, इतिहास और संस्कृति का संगम है ये ।
विश्व विख्यात,भव्य,अमरत्व का मेला है ये ।।

प्रत्येक बारह वर्षों में यह आयोजित होता ।
प्रयाग, हरिद्वार, उज्जैन और नासिक में मनाया जाता ॥

हुआ प्रारंभ इस परंपरा का, आदि गुरु शंकराचार्य से ।
हिंदू संस्कृति को सुदृढ़ करने और लोक कल्याण के भाव से॥

शाही स्नान लेने का क्रम बहुत पवित्र और अनुशासित होता ।
सर्व प्रथम नागा साधु तत्पश्चात अन्य श्रद्धालुओं को अवसर मिलता ।।

भारतीय संस्कृति और धार्मिक आस्था का अद्भुत संगम है ये।
मानवता की मूर्त सांस्कृतिक विरासत का सूचक है ये ।।

आओ मिलकर,इस विश्व धार्मिक समागम में सम्मिलित हो जाये ।
१४४ वर्षों बाद ,घटने वाले इस महाकुंभ के साक्षी बन जाये ।।

18. We, The People

The constitution, guiding light since it's inception,
Paved the way of India as a republic nation.

Crafted meticulously by distinguished and eminent
members,
Chief architect was the renowned scholar and reformer
B.R Ambedkar.

Every national symbol carries a narrative of profound
importance,
Thoughtfully chosen after digging history, its value and
relevance.

The president proudly takes salute at the RD Parade,
A parade showcasing India's unity and military heritage..

Vibrant tableaux from different states and UT
participate,
Evoking emotions of belongingness and pride for
cultural heritage.

Constitution of India was not a mere lawyer's document,
It was the expression of the will of The People and their
sentiment.

So let's celebrate this day with great fervour and passion,
As this day marked our footing in the world as a
fledgling nation.

19. Being Human

Our head is like a giant computer
Processing thoughts good and bad,
Inhale deeply and practice mindfulness
And push swiftly the pause tab.

Emotions ensure our survival
Otherwise we would have been a walking dead,
Vocalise them before they erupt
Leaving you frantic and depressed.

Mend relationship with your body
It's awful to have a hot body with a rotten mind,
Get enlightenment and a tight tush
By exercising the body and being kind.

Love comes in many packages
Experience it in different ways,
There is nothing like the perfect partner
So revel your married life in more vivid and memorable
ways.

Your kids are just an extension of you
Don't dump your stress on to them,
Invest in nurturing their innate talents
Refrain from blaming and patronising them.

Show compassion to self first and
Don't confuse it with selfishness,
As it builds resilience and stability
Creating trust, rapport and closeness.

Ignore and bury the battles in your head
It just ruins your present stage,
All humans are flawed in some ways
Accept, forgive and break free from the cage.

20. ऐसा भारत देश है मेरा

हुआ जन्म, जहां वेदों का,
तपोभूमि है, जो ऋषियों कि।।
तक्षशिला- नालंदा से,
"जगत गुरु" बन,शिक्षा बाँटी।।

गांधी, सुभाष, नेहरू जन्में जहां,
गोखले, तिलक,अहिल्याबाई ।।
सत्य-अहिंसा और साहस से,
अधीनता से, मुक्ति पाई ।।

शिक्षा के अवसर, समान जहां पर,
गुरू का स्थान, नहीं कम ईश्वर से ।।
रोज़गार हैं ,असंख्य यहाँ पर,
योग्यता पर ही,सब आँकें जाते।।

रंग बिरंगी वेशभूषा ,सबकी,
अनगिनत त्योहार, यहाँ पर ।।
सर्वोदयी समाज में रहते सब,
सौहार्द का ,भाव अपनाकर।।

भाँति भाँति के,लोग यहाँ पर,
पर देशप्रेम है ,एक सभी का।।
मातृभूमि पर, आँच आने पर,
हर देशप्रेमी का खून खौल उठता ।।

है गर्व हमें, इस लोकतंत्र पर,
जिसकी छाया में,हम रहते ।।
स्वावलंबन का गुण अपनाकर,
नित नए ,कीर्तिमान स्थापित करते ।।

विविधताओं ,को अपनाकर ही,
निर्माण हुआ इस राष्ट्र का है ।।
रहे तिरंगा ,सबसे ऊँचा ।।
लक्ष्य प्रत्येक, भारतीय ,का है ।।

युगों युगों से चली आ रही,
संस्कृति यह, महान है ।।
सत्य- अहिंसा, वसुदेव कुटुंबकम,
ही हमारी ,पहचान है ।।

आज उत्साह व स्वप्नों से भरित,
सारा यंगिसतान है ।।
विश्व शांति, तकनीकी, योग में,
अग्रणी हिन्दोस्तान है ।।

21. Rise Up

It's not easy being a woman in this perpetually changing
world ,
It takes a lot of pluck and spunk to hold that tiara and
swirl.

Don't let others take your politeness as your weakness,
As it encourages the bully to oppress and leave you
restless.

Stop pitying yourself and get rid of that delusion,
As new beginnings await once you face self-
confrontation.

Create a realistic life and shrug off those childhood
fantasies,
Accept the ordinary nature of life and recognise the
merits of pluralities.

Focus on your life rather snooping into others social
media life,

As it will cease the emulation and the real you will shine
and thrive.

Acquiring status and approval of others is not the true
path to happiness,
Rather it's the journey inwards which lead to personal
growth and self-consciousness.

Have courage to see your ugly side,Don't stay oblivious
to your own faults,
Become tolerant of your shortcomings and aware of the
hidden talents in your own vaults.

In this misanthropic world accept yourself as you are,
Develop self respect along with self esteem to win
everyday war.

Enrich your life by giving weightage to your individual
taste,
Be that mettlesome woman that makes no decisions in
haste.

Oh ...Dear Women !!
Break free from the shackles of working round the
clock,
Often give yourself a priority and let the repertoire of
unmet dreams unlock.